Yr 3

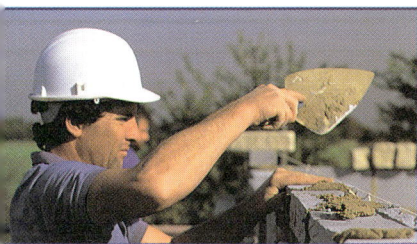

Building a House

Contents

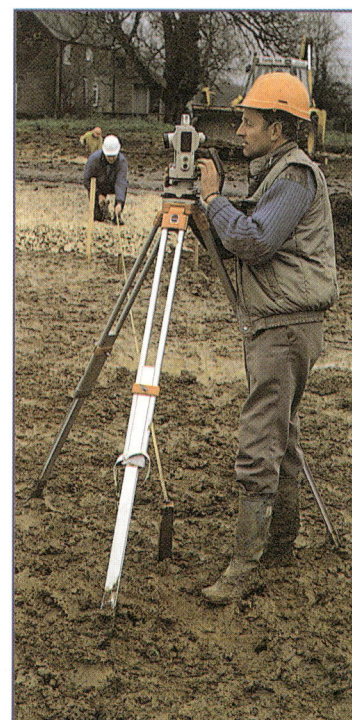

The building site

This field is empty now. In a year's time, Tom and Sarah will be living in a house here.

Tom and Sarah will be able to walk to school
from their new house. There won't be much traffic
in the new road, so they'll be able to play outside.
The shops are round the corner and the railway
station is only five minutes' walk.

The team

All kinds of people are needed to build a house.

Some of them plan the work before the building starts.

The builder buys the site and is in charge of the building work.

Some of them build the house.

The bricklayer does the brickwork.

The carpenter does the woodwork on the site.

The joiner does the woodwork in the workshop and later inside the house.

The electrician does the electrical work.

Inspectors check that the work has been done properly.

The plasterer puts plaster on the walls and ceilings.

The plumber does all the work to do with water and gas inside the house. He also puts in the central heating.

The decorator does the painting and decorating.

The roof tiler puts the tiles on the roof.

Planning the house

Before building can start, a lot of work has to be done. First the builder buys the land. Then he looks in a catalogue of house plans. He chooses a house and asks an architect to make drawings. The builder will use the drawings to build a house like the one in the catalogue.

The architect draws a plan of the house.

Building the house

The ground floor

When the plans are drawn the building work can begin.
First, a **digger** clears the site. It makes the ground level. The earth is put to one side so it can be used later.

The builder 'draws' a plan of the house on the ground. He uses string to show where the walls will go.

The digger digs **trenches** for the **foundations**. The workers pour in concrete. This makes a **footing** for the wall.

Walls and floors

The bricklayers start to build the walls. They use a **line**. This makes sure that the walls are straight.

Each outside wall is really two walls, called leaves. The leaves have a space between them, called a **cavity**.

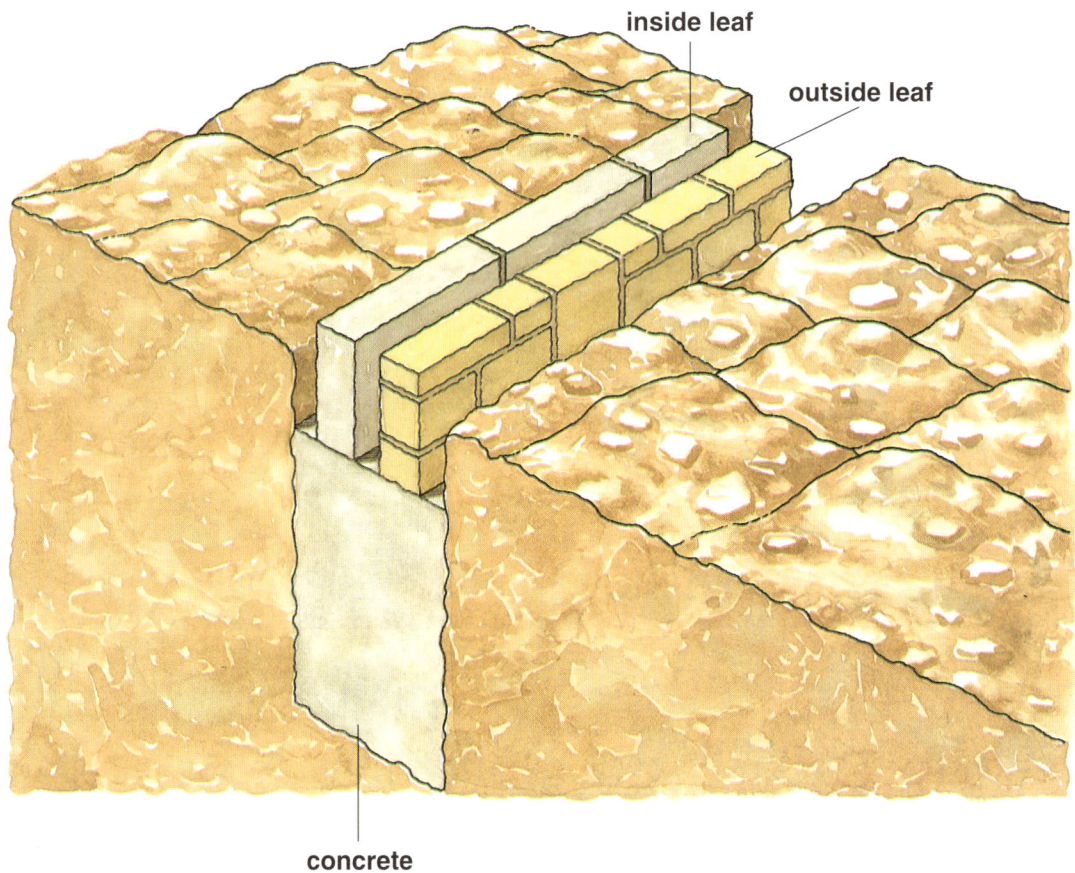

inside leaf

outside leaf

concrete

Then the floor is built. It is made up of many layers.

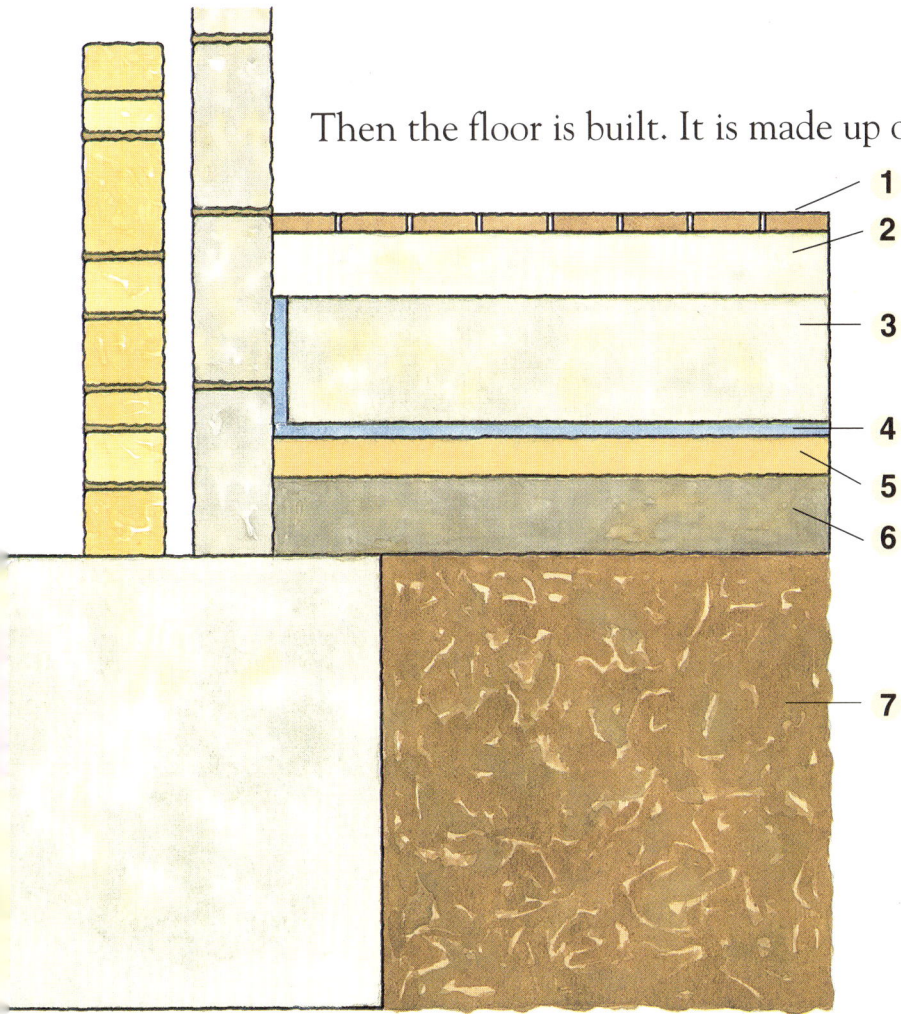

Key

1 Wooden floor – this isn't put in until later

2 Thin layer of concrete – this is called the 'screed' and is also added later

3 Concrete floor

4 Damp-proof course – a sheet of polythene which stops water from the ground coming up into the house

5 Smooth sand

6 Thick layer of broken stones and concrete – this is called the 'hard core'

7 Soil

Making the floor flat with a whacker

whacker

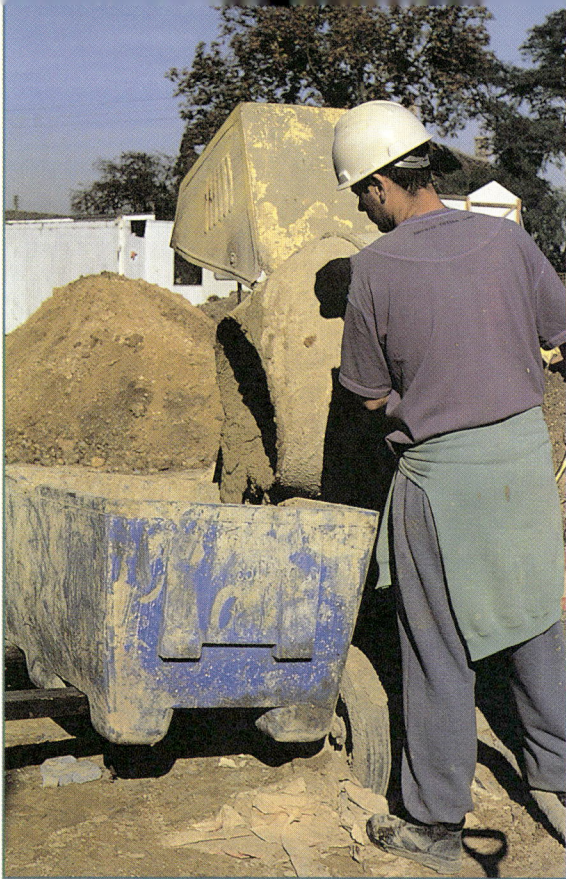
Mixing mortar in a cement mixer

The bricklayers carry on building the walls. They have to work fast in good weather. They can't work in rain or frost because wet weather can damage wet concrete.

They stick the bricks and blocks together with mortar. Mortar is a kind of concrete. The bricks in this house are made of stone. In other houses the bricks are made of clay. The pattern of bricks is called a bond. Bonding makes the wall stronger.

Here are some different bonds to look out for:

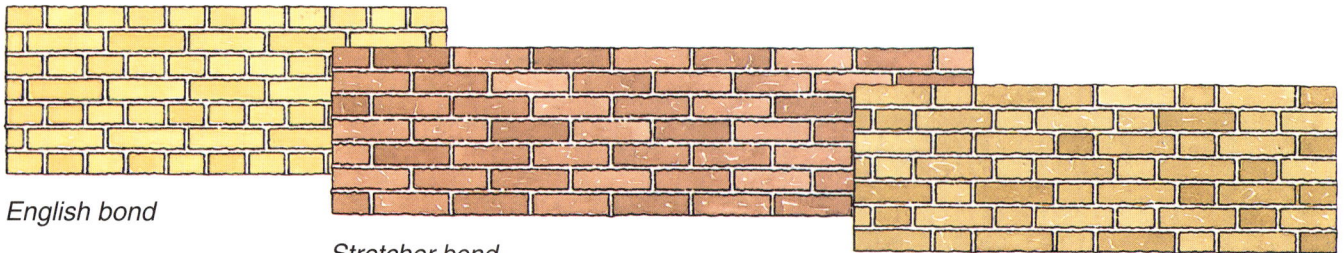
English bond

Stretcher bond

Flemish bond

The inspector comes round to check the work.

Doors and windows

The door-frames and window-frames arrive on a lorry. The bricklayers have left spaces for them in the walls. They finish building the wall round the frames.

They place a piece of concrete, called a lintel, over each door and window. This carries the weight of the bricks on top.

This is how the door-frame is fixed to the wall.

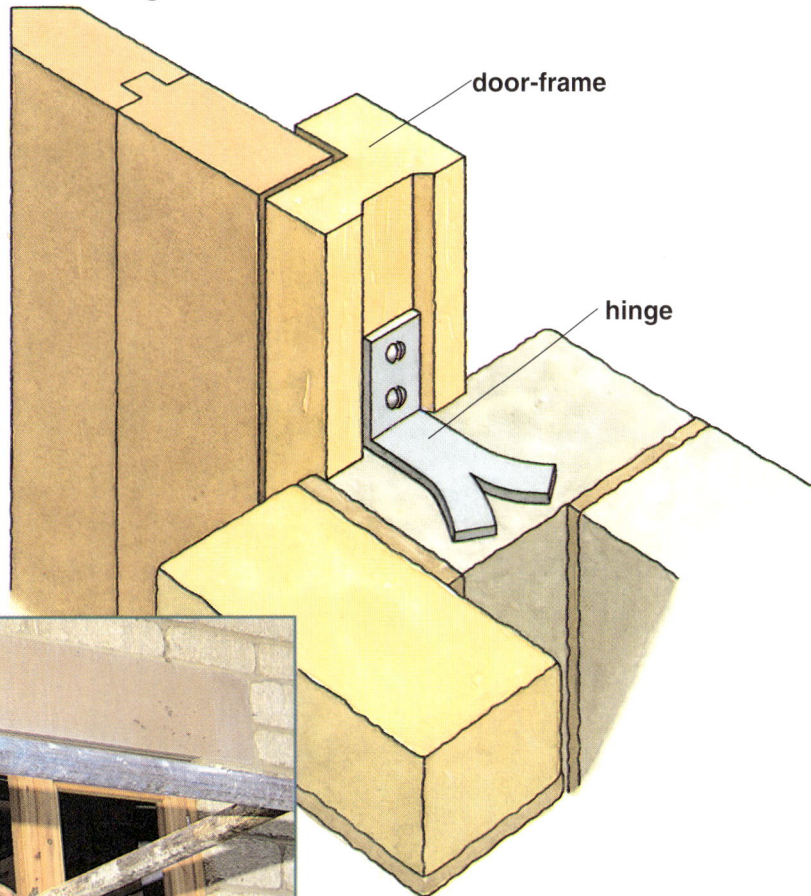

lintel

door-frame

hinge

The wall is now too high for the bricklayers. It's time to build the **scaffolding**. The scaffolders tie the scaffolding to the walls.

11

The inside walls

The bricklayer builds the main wall inside, using concrete blocks.

The electrician cuts a little trench in the wall. This is for the electricity wires and the light switch. Then the wall is plastered.

The carpenters build the other inside walls.

First, they build a wooden frame. Later they cover the wall with plasterboard. Plasterboard is a stiff sheet of plaster, covered in paper. Spaces are left for the doorways and inside windows.

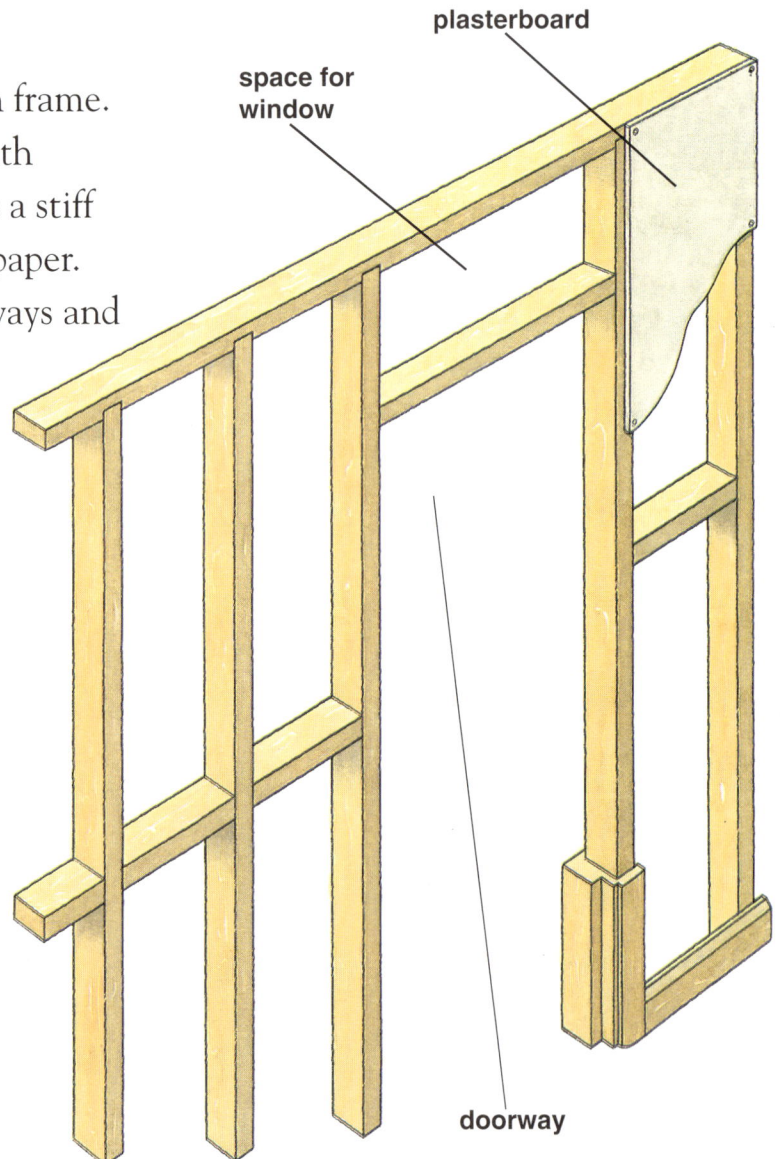

plasterboard

space for window

doorway

The first floor

The carpenters place wooden beams from one outside wall to the other. The beams are called joists.

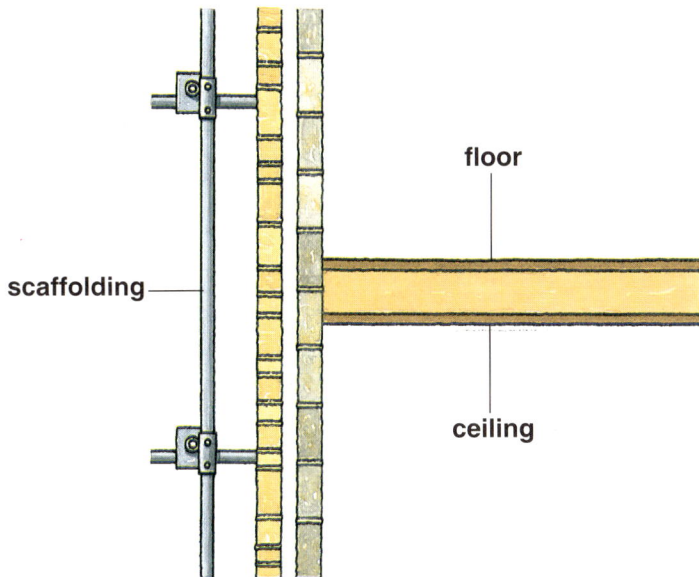

joists

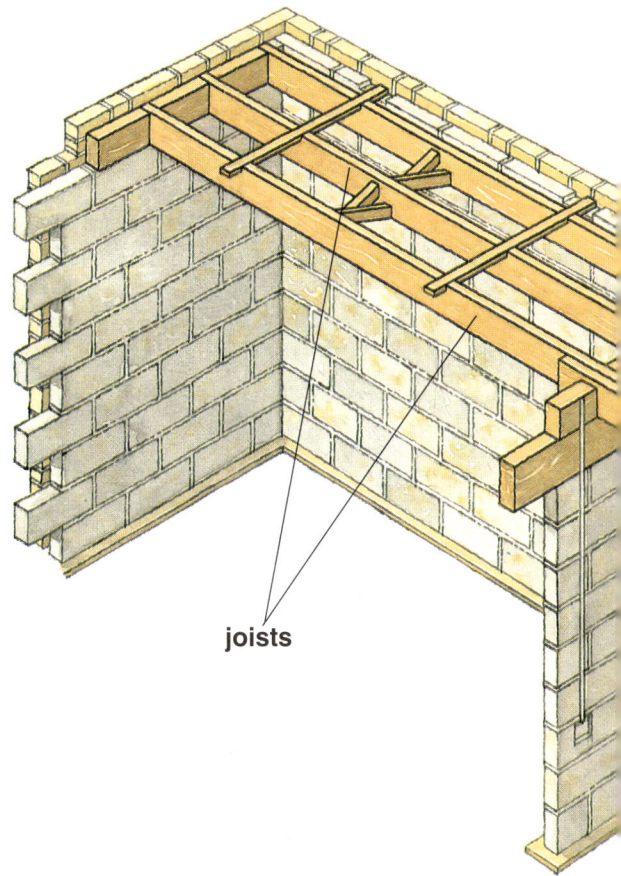

scaffolding

floor

ceiling

The ceiling of the ground floor is nailed to the under-side of the joists. The floor of the bedrooms sits on top of the joists.

Holes are left in the floor for the staircase and for the heating and water pipes.

Building the roof

The carpenters build the wooden frame for the roof.

The tiler nails a sheet of **felt** to the roof.

rafters

Then the tiler nails on strips of wood,
called **tile battens**, to the felt.

14

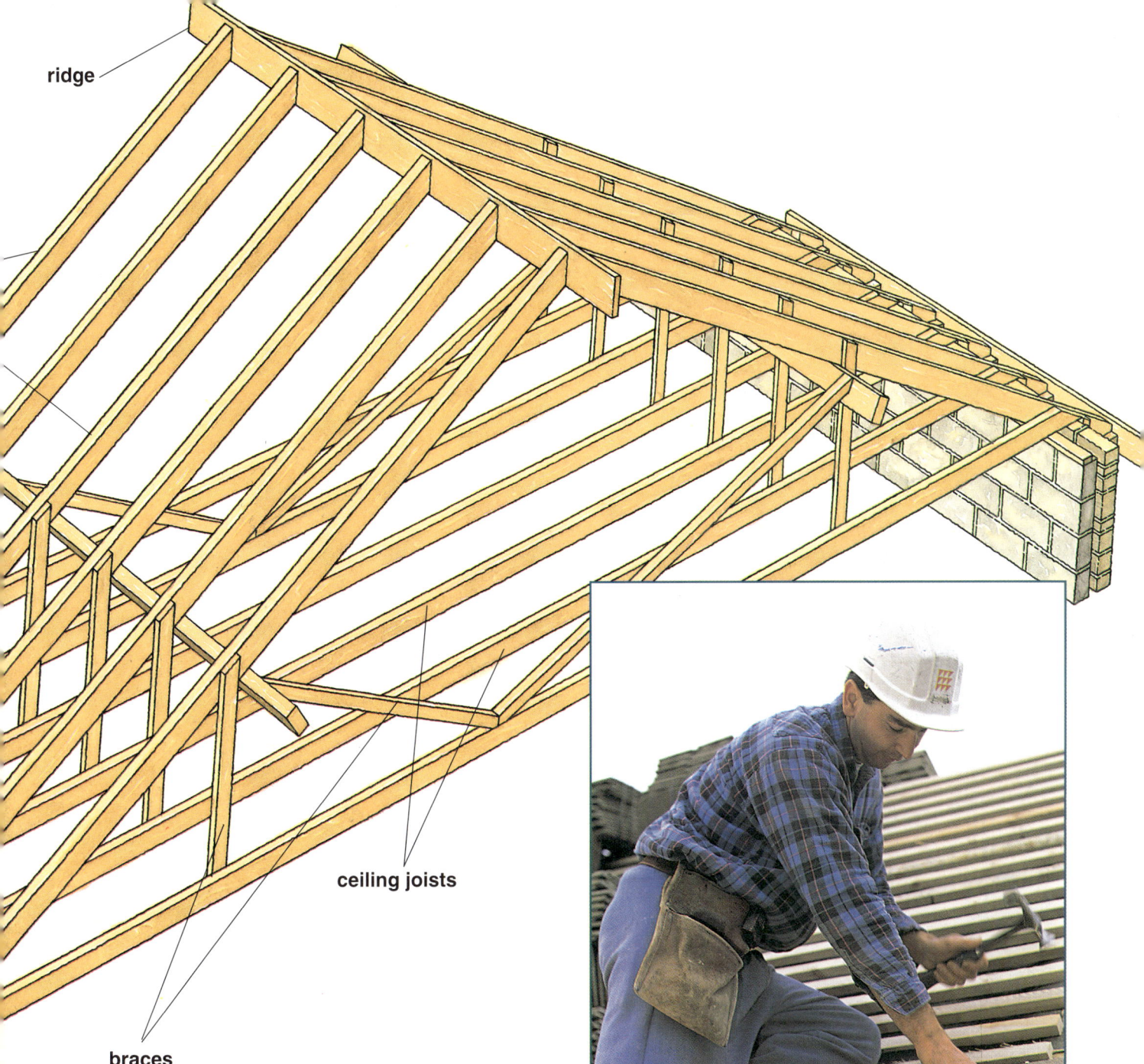

ridge

braces

ceiling joists

Tiles are nailed on top of the **tile battens**.
This keeps out the rain. The tiles overlap,
to cover the nails.

Water, gas and electricity

The shell of the house is ready. Before the builders do any more work they tidy up. It's now time to put in the things that make life comfortable:

- running water, for washing and cooking
- drainage pipes, to take the dirty water away
- gas, for cooking and heating
- electricity, for the lights and the machines
- roof insulation, to keep the heat in.

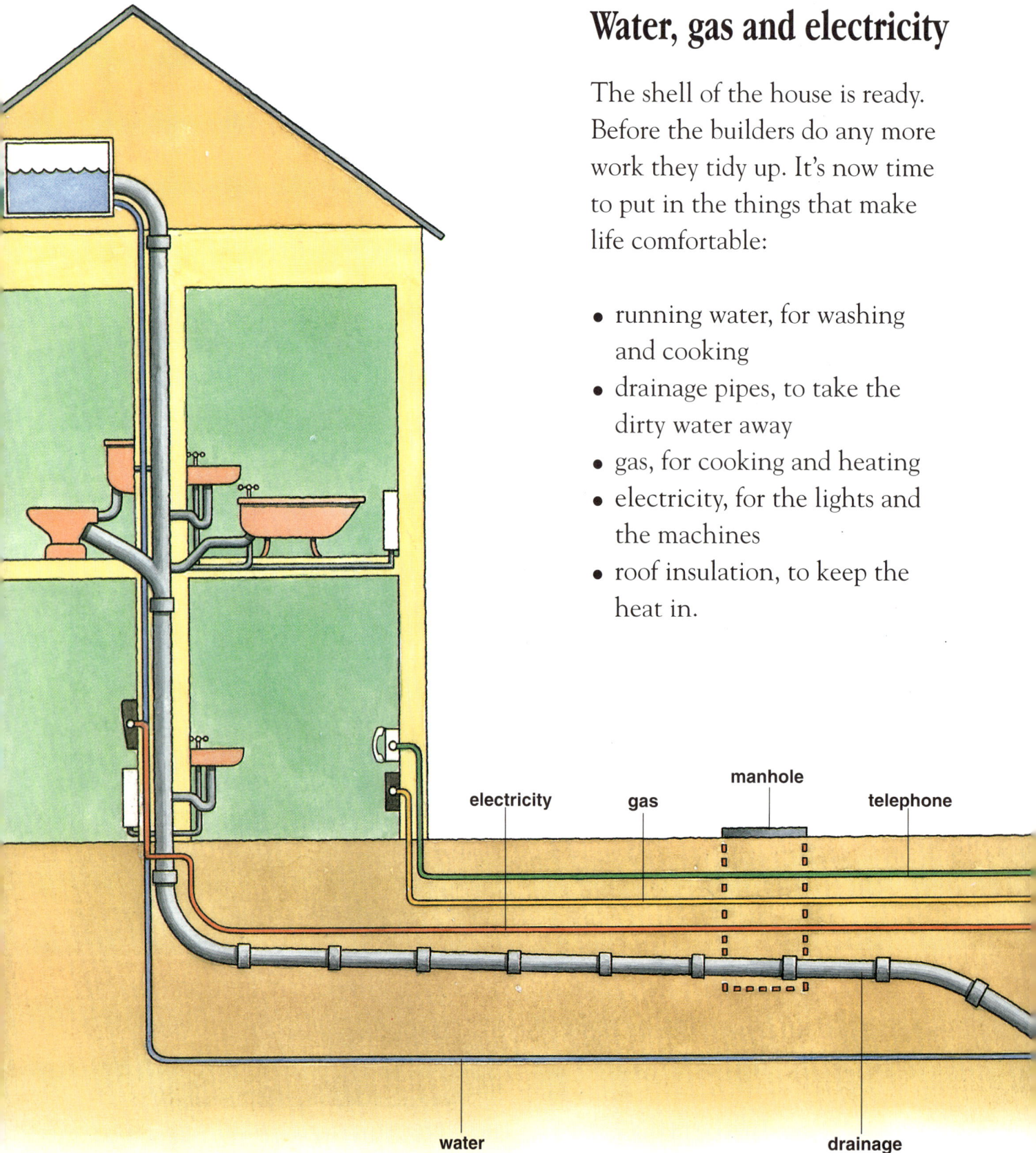

electricity

gas

manhole

telephone

water

drainage

Finishing the inside

Now that everything is tidy, there is a lot of inside work to do. The suppliers have to make sure they bring the fittings in good time.

Fitting the toilet

Fixing on door handles

Painting the ceiling

Putting a socket on the wall

Tiling the kitchen

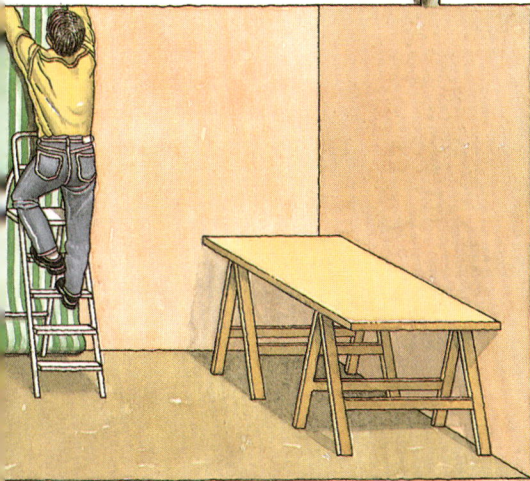

Painting the walls

Finishing the outside

There is quite a lot of work to do outside, too.

Laying the lawn

Building the fence

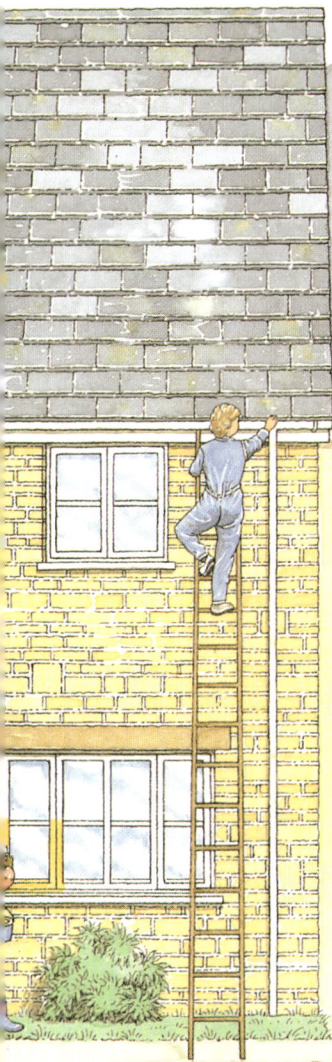

How the house grew

The site – 1st September

Preparing the foundations – 3rd January

Building the ground floor – 10th March

Building the first floor – 15th March

Building the roof – 12th June

The finished house – 6th September

Glossary

cavity

the gap between the inside and outside leaves of a wall

digger

a machine for digging trenches

felt

a thick waterproof sheet on the roof– the tiles go on top of it

footing

the concrete on which the outside walls stand

foundation

all the wall and footings under the ground

line

a piece of string that shows the bricklayer where to build the walls

scaffolding

a frame of steel pipes round a building– it carries planks for walling on so that bricklayers can work high up

tile battens

strips of wood on the roof– the tiles are nailed to them

trench

a wide, straight hole in the ground made with a digger

Index